Brilliance
UNBOXED

For Lisa,

May your brilliance in every way ♡

Jo Gifford

ISBN: 978-1-913590-02-4 (paperback)
ISBN: 978-1-913590-03-1 (ebook)

Published by The Unbound Press

Foreword

I have a secret.

No, not my trashy stadium rock fetish - I see the brilliance in others.

I see how to articulate that special blend of brilliance that only YOU have, so you can crack on with making an impact, creating your life your way, and cranking up your income.

So, what's *your* pure magic?

If you don't know it yet, we can discover it here together.

If you do know it, let's continue to play into possibility and explore.

It serves no one to hide your brilliance; it's not polite to play it down, or rude to be amazing.

You are inherently awesome. However you choose to shine, own it, claim it and live it.

Shining doesn't mean being loud, inauthentic or brash.

It's permission to be you, wholeheartedly.

You got this.

She-she-she-shine on Giff Xoxox

Contents

Introduction

Never speak in absolute terms, Jo, unless you're speaking about how happy, wonderful and amazing you are.

Or, when speaking of absolute terms.

Totally,

The Universe

This book is for you.

It's also for me.

It's a love letter to all of us, and an invitation to take a journey into your brilliance - what it is, how to find it, how to use it, and how to develop it.

The moment I knew I had to write this book, I laughed.

I was driving through the countryside on a bright December morning, a smile wide on my face as I chuckled along with the Big U - the Universe/God/Source, however you prefer to refer to that Quantum Field of awesome that is all around us - and I realised with a joyous surrender, 'of COURSE! My whole life so far has led to this book, this moment, this conversation, and this work'.

How simple it all seems when we connect the dots.

And yet, how complicated we - and by we I wholeheartedly mean this human right here writing to you - can make it.

I have been using the word 'brilliance' for some time in my work as a designer, writer, consultant and personal branding mentor.

I created a process called 'Brilliance Ignition', a set of behaviours and habits that set the scene for inspiration, innovation, and inspired thought (more on that in the book later).

I always referred to brilliance as being that mysterious, magical set of character traits, ideas, skills, gifts and behaviours that only you have.

Your brilliance is where you feel in your power, where you live and act as the best version of yourself.

It's also where the biggest impact is for those around you.

Perhaps you know it as your zone of genius, or your unique gift, but I see it as those things and much more -which we will explore together in this book.

A large part of my body of work has been to help amazing people see their own brilliance, to step into the confidence of knowing what it is, and to get that message out to the world.

My super power is seeing the brilliance in others; I can unearth, during conversations and work together, the exact magic ingredients that an individual brings to the world, and how they stand apart from others.

It felt easy to me, yet the results for my clients were nothing short of transformational.

I saw women gain such velocity with their message and work that their work sparked movements, and their businesses and service to the world blew up in a way that surprised us all.

I saw the changes in body posture, in how they spoke and presented themselves, in how they were thinking.

I saw, in effect, people change in front of my eyes.

These wonderful women were making connections that were sparking something magical inside their very souls, and their lives were changed forever.

Of course, this was always from a personal branding and marketing approach at first, but then something I hadn't expected began to happen; the more I worked with my clients doing this work, the more I realised how many of these brilliant women were afraid to step into their brilliance.

I realised how many of them - how many of *us* - had been holding back their message and their voices for their whole lives.

There are many, many reasons for this, and we will explore them together as we go through these pages. I am certain you will recognise yourself in more than a few of the scenarios we will cover.

Sometimes we don't even realise we are holding back. After all, we are doing all the 'right' things, we have followed the 'right' paths, and we are living a life we thought we wanted. But what if there is more to it? What if you allowed yourself to truly explore what your unique gift is, and to lead from that place in your life?

Well, that might just be a wonderful thing, and who knows where it might lead.

I recommend that you delve into this book and get a feel for the words on the pages, then come back and revisit the parts that really struck a chord with you to go deeper.

You will hear my story, and we will meet other wonderful women along the way who are unboxing their brilliance just like you, and what the experience looked like for them.

We have resources to help you go deeper, and a community of people ready to greet you and go on this journey with you.

The book has several journal prompts as we work through the pages. I personally believe there is immense power in putting pen to paper as we process information, so I have included some moments for you to pause and reflect.

I am so delighted this book found its way into your hands. I know we were meant to hang out in this space together.

So, we are about to embark on an adventure, you and I (I LOVE adventures!).

We are about to start unboxing your brilliance. So, well done. You have taken the first step by having this book in your world.

The next steps will be different for each of you, but the most magical part is to just start.

Just dive in. Let your process, your unfolding, and unboxing begin.

Look out for signs as you do this.

Signposts are everywhere to support you: that song on the radio, that comment from a friend, that article that landed on the desk/digital equivalent thereof.

It's like a personally hand drawn version of dot-to-dot starts to appear for you to follow as soon as you say yes to your mission.

The universe is rather good at placing bite-sized clues for soul level challenges, so we never have to be overwhelmed by an avalanche of discovery, emotion, development or insights.

Also, this is kinda a lifelong thing. Yep. Sorry/not sorry.

We have so many layers to uncover, to expand into, to own, revel in and joyously dance with, that the brilliance unboxing just never stops.

It is my wish that we all just become more mindful of it, more in tune with it, and to love every moment of (re)discovering just how brilliant you are.

As we begin our brilliance voyage together, I want to set out some premises, peep at some assumptions, and take a meander through some unbound boundaries as we go.

Let's start with what I am NOT, shall we?

I am NOT:

- A philosopher

- A sociologist

- An expert in confidence

- A religious icon of any sort

But, I AM:

- A human being with thoughts, opinions and experience

- A creative thinker

- Experienced in working with people through their blocks of sharing their brilliance

- Allowing myself to speak about this stuff intuitively

This book is a combination of academic insights, qualitative feedback, personal experiences, and a hefty dose of intuition, sprinkled across the pages like a spray gun of glitter got let off (and in my house, that's a very plausible and possible thing to happen, happily).

I will be pulling from stats and facts, citing the work of others before me, but also flying with what feels good too.

So as you read, take what works for you and leave what doesn't.

I promise I won't be offended.

You are here for a reason, Brilliant One.

You are exploring brilliance because you feel drawn to it, so whatever jumps out at you, follow that thread and see where it takes you.

The process of unboxing your brilliance happens at a different pace for us all, and there are no hard and fast rules, no 'shoulds', 'goals' or actions to take other than building awareness and feeling into what you - and specifically you - feel drawn to explore more.

Alrighty.

Let's dive in.

Let's make space for your brilliance and begin to unbox it together, shall we?

Jo xo

Brilliance Unboxed

What is brilliance, anyway?

What is my genius?
How can I bring forth my genius in a way that serves others and myself at the same time?

Those who have the courage to discover and bring forth their genius break through to unparalleled heights of productivity and life satisfaction.

— Gay Hendricks, The Big Leap

Growing up, I was the archetypal good girl and overachiever.

My grades in school were excellent. I got 9 A's in my GCSE's, ABB at A-Level, then went on to do my degree in 2-D design, an MA in Design Management, and a career I adored in Graphic Design. I was ticking all the boxes on the achievement route planner I had somehow formed in my head as 'the right way' - maybe you had one of those imaginary route planners too?

I absolutely LOVED school (learning has always been a passion of mine), I adored my undergrad and postgrad degrees, and I was thriving in my career.

Everything looked rosy on paper.

To the outside world, it looked as if everything was working out. Everything was going to plan, externally.

Internally? Well, that was another conversation altogether.

Being a good girl has many issues; bound up within that behaviour and mindset is an override setting on your soul. When you aim to please other people and not yourself, when you seek approval outside of yourself to feel validated, you forget the internal navigation system within.

Our inner GPS is an incredibly powerful thing. Without it, we lose our connection to who we really are; to who the soul is behind the achievements, the grades, the status, the academic rewards, and the list of goals being ticked off with a frantic mania.

I defined myself, and my brilliance (or lack thereof), by my achievements. This is a non-starter for many reasons, not least because there is always someone more accomplished, there is always another ladder to climb, and you are never, ever enough right now.

Being brilliant, for me, meant doing all the things, ticking all the boxes, being seen to be awesome.

It took me a long, long time to realise that I was looking for validation outside of myself.

My drive was about being loved and acknowledged, not about working on things that lit me up or being guided by my soul. My 'brilliance' wasn't at a soul-cell level. It was shallow, judgemental, subjective, transient, and hollow.

I had inherited, as we all do, an outline of what being me should be.

I didn't question it for many years, and I didn't see that the tracks I was on weren't placed by me, ordered by me, or even given a cursory glance of approval by me - at least not consciously.

To step into true brilliance is to undo, unpick, unpack - to unbox - all the stuff you didn't ask for, and to start filling up with intentional guidance and exploration.

That, right there, is a glimmer of light that starts to make things exciting.

Since we are unboxing brilliance here, it's a great opportunity to check back in with what it actually is.

Maybe you already have an opinion formed about what brilliance means for you, or maybe what it has meant for you in the past . Now is a great time to revisit that definition and check back in with how you feel about it. In fact, it's perfect, divine timing for you to redefine what it means for you.

Maybe you think that someone is 'brilliant' if they are intelligent, accomplished, knowledgeable, witty, or kind.

Maybe you have certain standards as to what 'brilliance' means, and a benchmark of reaching that standard.

Maybe you see it as dharma, or 'zone of genius', maybe you think of it as being your soul purpose, or your calling in life.

For me, it's all of those things, and none of them, at once.

The Oxford English Dictionary tells us that 'brilliance' is either 'Intense brightness of light' or 'Exceptional talent or intelligence'.

Well, here's how I see brilliance; I see it as that wonderful, magical, unique blend of your personality, your quirks, weirdness, your humour, your experience, and your skills.

I see that brightness of light as something that only *you* have.

It's your you-ness.

It's those moments when you feel so totally, unquestionably you.

It's when you are in your power.

Brilliance for us in the context of this book doesn't necessarily mean having the greatest academic mind.

We don't need to be anything other than who we are already - the problem is, we often don't really know who that is.

I call this the Personal Power Paradigm.

I have used this framework in my work to help people connect with their own unique lens on the world from the context of a personal brand and message, but truly the Personal Power Paradigm is relevant to all of us in discovering our brilliance.

It's the baseline of what makes you awesome - and yes, we are going to need to start getting used to the fact that acknowledging you are awesome is part of the brilliance unboxing.

It's also a roadmap to discovering how you tick, how you work, rest, and play at your best.

It's the manual to YOU, and to finding more of what makes you feel in that incredible power.

Often we only realise that we aren't connected to our brilliance because we feel 'off'.

Sometimes we don't know what our brilliance is until we know, viscerally, what it is *not,* and this was certainly the case for me.

Back in 2005, I was 29 years old. I was in a great job at a London design agency with a beautifully bespoke dual role as Senior Designer and New Business Development Manager.

I had an East End loft flat in Hackney that I loved, I had a 'great' (or so I thought) relationship, I was studying part time for my MA in Design Management, I had friends, income - I had everything I had strived for. On paper, at least.

So when I began to feel crippling anxiety, tiredness that would not shift, and experiencing panic attack after panic attack it shook me to the core.

I was capable. I was a manager at work, a 'doer' in my life and social circles, I had ticked all the boxes. What on earth could be wrong?

My soul was crying, *that* was what was wrong.

My soul knew, at a deep, cellular level, that I wasn't living in a way that nurtured my very essence.

I was disconnected from my spirit; I was living so much in my ego and my head that I overrode all the systems and signals my body was giving me.

I drank through it. I over exercised through it. I signed up for counselling, I changed my diet, I did All The Right Things, but I still couldn't shake the crushing fatigue, constant sickness, and crippling fear that I was about to lose everything I had just achieved.

Even as I write this, I picture the younger me and just want to hug her and tell her it's going to be ok.

With the wisdom of a 42 year old future version of me, I can see now so very clearly that I needed to learn the art of self care, of advocating for myself, of truly seeing myself for the glorious bundle of brilliance I was, and I am. I just didn't know how.

So I carried on *doing.*

I tried, I pushed harder, I went to work with migraines and travelled home every evening throwing up with exhaustion. I didn't understand what was happening to me, or that these terrifying symptoms were the cries of my body and soul for attention, for nourishment beyond the multiple supplements and smoothies - to go within, and to truly discover who I am.

For me, it took for me to be broken to start to listen.

Of course, being 'broken' was, in my head at least, a failure.

But as we shall see, sometimes the very thing that we think of as failure is often the edge to our brilliance.

But for now, let's talk about YOU.

Today I want for you to think about how everything that makes you a complete and utter failure is actually what makes you totally brilliant.

It's also a huge insight when building your personal brand, but that's a side benefit to a core understanding.

I know so many people whose so-called 'failures' have enabled them to work and operate from their edge, to help them work in a unique and magical way that adds more value to their clients.

Here's what I mean:

I am a huge fan of letting tech do the heavy lifting where possible, and my daisy chain apps and smart working techniques are something I am well known for - but not because I am a Silicon Valley-bearded-hipster-genius.

Nope.

Learning this stuff came from running my design agency and working as a freelance writer and being a mum of young twins.

Having two babies at once is, it turns out, PRETTY FRICKIN' TIRING (albeit awesome), and I needed to work out how to manage my clients, my work and my sanity - so I amped up my app game.

Similarly, I am vocal and open about working and living with chronic illnesses (yes, those warning signs developed into much more, as we shall see later in this book).

I have designed my life and work around these now, so I know a lot about how to work to your strengths, how to focus, and how to work smart.

I also use leverage as a tool in my work, and I love to reach as many people as possible by using content I have already created and interacting with clients online. This means the output of my brain is available for clients even when I am sleeping/doing the school run/hanging out with my cat.

So how about you?

Unboxing your brilliance can start with the simplest step of just realising that other perspectives are available. That your greatest weakness just might be one of your strengths.

Stay curious. Find what feels good, as Adriene would say (any other *Yoga with Adriene* fans out there?).

Unbox your brilliance bit by bit, and enjoy the unboxing as you go.

Once we begin to unbox our brilliance from the narratives of normalcy, new opportunities and ideas arise.

Staying open to them is the key.

I want you to embrace the glorious permission that this gives you to think in new ways.

In my experience, when you start to open up to alternative ways of earning income, or of viewing your skills and how they fit together, it's truly expansive; your juices start to flow, possibility flows through every part of you, and you start to see connections, ideas and potential everywhere.

That openness is delicious.

I want you to really feel that new connection to 'other'; to untold social narratives, to new horizons, ideas, ways of being, thoughts, people, opportunity. All of it.

The best part is that your renewed excitement raises your vibration and literally pulls in more signposts for brilliance from the Universe (Or the Big U, as I often refer to it).

When you start unboxing your brilliance and feeling that sense of elation and potential, the world around you rewards you by sprinkling more bread crumbs for you to follow.

That amazing conversation you had with a stranger in the café that sparked a new idea?

The book you stumbled upon in the junk shop that leapt out and inspired you?

That radio programme that spoke directly to you?

As you will find again and again on your unboxing of brilliance , the signposts are everywhere.

As we start, make like Hansel and Gretel, and keep following those breadcrumbs.

Journal prompts:

- What definition would you give to brilliance right now?

- Who would you nominate as someone who is brilliant? (this could be someone you know personally, or a celebrity figure, past or present).

- When do you feel in your power?

- How do you feel about acknowledging that you are powerful?

- If you think about the word 'failure' - what images does that conjure in your mind? How does it make you feel?

Brilliance Unboxed

Seeing your brilliance

Your secret blessing, Jo, is that no matter where you go in time and space, you only ever have to be yourself - as courageous, vulnerable, bold, or afraid as you may feel - to find yourself amongst friends. So loved, The Universe
(Notes from the Universe, Mike Dooley)

Let's talk about who you are. Your identity. Your you-ness. It's something we create and curate all the time by choosing where to shop, what we post, who we hang out with, how we spend our time.

When do you feel TRULY like you are 'you'? What is happening in those moments?

For me, I feel like myself when at a Morning Gloryville event or on an art gallery mooch on an Autumn day, after my Saturday yoga class in that magically grounded afterglow. Or when cooking with tunes on, creating something with my daughters, reading on a lazy Sunday, being with friends drinking gin, and many other moments.

But being you becomes diluted in life all too easily.

We may occupy many roles within one lifetime. I am a daughter, a friend, a sister, a partner, a Mum, a colleague, a cousin, a niece, a professional, a morning raver, an artist, a writer, a designer, a meditator, a cook, a driver, an ear for others.

It's likely that within most of the roles we play, the tendency is to go with the flow of that façade, and to do what is required of us in that moment - whether it's making dinner for the family, dealing with school correspondence, adhering to deadlines, or listening to a friend in need.

All too often, we realise that no-one has actually asked how we are for hours, maybe days, or weeks (sound familiar?).

We are in the cycle of 'getting on with it', a phrase used to push aside our own needs as a badge of honour and stoicism. I am British, and the 'stiff upper lip' ideology passed down in our society is still very present, somehow woven into the fabric of many conversations.

I am a keen advocate for seeking help when needed.

Some years ago when I embarked upon a fresh block of counselling appointments, I realised how oddly indulgent it felt to have someone purely focussed on me and my needs for a whole hour. It felt like the first time I had been seen and heard in far, far too long, and it was so very needed. It's this kind of nurturing inner enquiry and feedback system that we need to build into as many relationships and areas of our lives as possible. To be able to reflect, evolve and grow regularly is incredibly powerful, and a brilliance squad will help you to do just that.

Often we inherit people around us - maybe family members or a social circle - whose presence in our lives is subtractive. They don't nurture us, see us for who we are, and nor do they have a burning desire to start doing so, either. I will talk more about how to deal with people like this later on in the book (incidentally, when you start owning and unboxing your brilliance, you naturally upgrade your circles around you to a much more supportive squad).

The result of inherited networks over soul-led, brilliance fuelled connections and conversations, is that we can get stuck in a way of operating that doesn't suit who we are as awesome human beings.

I now have friends all across the world that I can reach out to and be truly, 100 percent myself with. Whether I reach out with a call or message to celebrate a win, to seek feedback or advice, or simply to ugly cry and ask that space be held for me, I am surrounded by truly amazing, insightful and compassionate people; people who dare to challenge me with love and empathy, who hold space for whatever I need, which of course I also do for them.

It takes courage to start doing the work of brilliance unboxing. The pay-off, however, is huge, tangible and quick to see.

As you start to unbox your brilliance, it challenges those around you to shine a light on who they are. A ripple effect of your soul reclamation process is that an incredibly powerful sequence of events may start and act as a trigger to affect many changes around you - some tiny and undetectable, some like pouring glitter over the elephant in the room and asking it to do a tap dance under a spotlight.

Particles change when they are observed. We are no different; we run faster when someone is watching, we do more when someone is aware of our progress. But, as you unbox your brilliance, be mindful of the audiences you choose.

Be your own observer. Be the unicorn in the corner, happy to be acknowledged and seen by yourself, for all that you are.

Cliques come and go. Who and what is in vogue changes.

There is a huge sense of joy and happiness in acknowledging yourself, and not the approval of others.

Be your own cheering squad.

And when someone really sees you? That's a huge bonus but not the goal.

Being seen is something that we all crave as human beings.

To be truly seen and acknowledged for all that we are, for who we are at at a cellular, soul level.

As you embark on your brilliance unboxing, my hope for you is that you learn to see yourself - for there is no greater gift than to be your own champion, your in-house advocate and illustrious, neon-signed leader of your own life.

Journal Prompts:

What does being seen mean to you?

Who have you always longed to be seen by?

What would it mean for you to see yourself?

When are you yourself?

How does it feel?

How might you feel that more often?

Braving Brilliance

'We are complex beings who wake up every day and fight against being labeled and diminished with stereotypes and characterisations that don't reflect our fullness. Yet when we don't risk standing on our own and speaking out, when the options laid before us force us into the very categories we resist, we perpetuate our own disconnection and loneliness. When we are willing to risk venturing into the wilderness, and even becoming our own wilderness, we feel the deepest connection to our true self and to what matters the most.'

— **Brené Brown,** *Braving the Wilderness: The Quest for True Belonging and the Courage to Stand Alone*

Brilliance isn't always about living in the light.

In fact, it's in the darkness that we find the duality of our shadows, and the clue to what can become our edge.

It's an act of courage to begin unboxing your brilliance and to dare to make an enquiry into your very essence.

As we unpack parts of ourselves - our actions, thoughts, deeds, approaches, experiences - the process can be as painful as it is enlightening and up-lifting.

It's not for the faint of heart, but nor is there a time limit around this stuff.

Working on uncovering who we are to live life fully is a journey of peeling back the layers - some layers are exciting to look at, some can bring up challenges, but all the layers serve a purpose of moving us forward.

Aside from the journey of moving through what you find, there is often a great deal of courage needed to be able to 'be' with yourself, for all that it means.

There are multiple categories under which we might file our sense of "being" - 'mother', 'partner', 'entrepreneur', 'daughter', 'invisible illness advocate', 'creative', to use some of mine as examples - are all locked and loaded with pre-written narratives on what each one means about us.

It's all too easy to gather up all the pre-loaded stories, assumptions, and society prescribed identities, and end up with a whole character that doesn't, in fact, belong to us at all.

Maybe you have experienced that clawing, gnawing feeling that your life ticks all the boxes, but doesn't 'feel' right?

When we cross off the checklists handed to us by our peers, culture, family - very often curated internally by ourselves, without questioning the validity or authenticity of the goals we spend our lives trying to achieve - we go into autopilot and cut off the connection to our soul.

Ouch.

I know this only too well.

My soul had been trying to make itself heard for a long time.

Throughout my childhood I had illnesses that would last for long periods of time; from bouts of the flu that would last for weeks to recurring ear infections, tonsillitis, hip problems, all sorts.

I spent a long time needing to rest and be looked after, a theme that would come back later in life like a reprised character from a movie that goes rogue.

At the age of 19 I began experiencing excruciating pain in my abdomen and extreme tiredness.

Over 7 years I would seek to find out what this pain was, and how to deal with the impact on my life. I finally got a diagnosis of endometriosis. Chronic fatigue and fibromyalgia followed over the coming years to coexist in a cacophony of pain and exhaustion - but one heck of a journey to the abyss of my soul and and back up again.

It's no secret that you often find your edge in the darkest of times.

For me, mental and physical health experiences have led me to places that have left me raw, broken, and feeling so far away from brilliance that to connect the two concepts just felt jarringly impossible - a cosmic joke of opposites.

From being bed bound with chronic fatigue syndrome, fibromyalgia and endometriosis while raising a young family, to the horror of postnatal depression and psychosis; from depressive episodes that lingered and threatened to take up residence and rot away my soul to anxiety, to the hot flash of a panic attack and the despair of my own mind and body letting me down.

Each time I have been brought to my knees in humble, terrifying surrender, I have found new opportunities to thrive; to re-wire, re-design and reconnect in a whole new way.

Like roots rising from the mess and dust of shattered concrete and rubble, those trails of promise bring new life.

With every edge comes experience, of course.

With every fear is empathy and understanding, even when amid the fiery knot of emotions we can't always see it.

I learned about smart working and tech power moves when I had to leverage time between being an exhausted mum of twins, running a design agency, and freelancing as a writer and blogger. Time and energy were limited. I had to get creative. Now, my knowledge of productivity and smart working is part of the unique mix I bring to my clients and project work. It's part of my edge.

I learned about remote agile working by needing to re-design how my energy was spent in a day; travel and energy drains out, smart working in.

I learned to leverage time with webinars, online courses, joint ventures and affiliate projects by needing to find a way to make the most of limited time and energy.

My edge - illness, time constraints and juggling as a working parent - meant I had to adapt, learn, evolve and grow.

But guess what?

Leaning into growth serves you well, and my clients and audience gain immensely from my experiments into re-designing the pieces of my puzzle and shifting my reality. I also began to effortlessly attract people who needed me and my work because of my experiences, not in spite of it.

When we dare to be real, raw, and honest, our brilliance emerges to serve others in ways we could not have planned out on a vision board.

There have been many times recently in my own life, where I have planned, set visions, goals and targets, but the week, month, or year has thrown me about in some turbulence of plot twist life curveballs. Often, when I have dared to surrender, to stay in the moment, to be truly me and not stress about what 'should' be, or where those goals or targets were, I achieved and gained more than I could ever have imagined.

Planning and aiming for goals can be amazing, and a powerful way to create a wonderful life.

For me, brilliance is about rolling with those plot twists, staying present, and being open to magic along the way. I invite you to stay open to possibilities too.

Unboxing the layers and finding bruises

There is always more to unbox as each layer lovingly discards a crumpled, beautifully unwrapped gift the deeper we go.

It often surprises me that every time I feel like I have reached a new level of unboxedness, of living authentically as me and being grounded in my brilliance, the expanse of rawness, deep scars, and untapped conscious streams can feel exhausting, tumultuous, traumatic, and sometimes limiting.

If for every action there is an equal and opposite reaction, then it would also follow that for every expansion there is an equally impactful retraction; that for every journey of breaking down boxes and moving onwards to growth, there is a deeper retrieval of forgotten mind patterns, latent neural pathways, and dormant darkness.

Discovery shines the light on a whole lifetime of mess that you chucked into the cupboard, but suddenly, the cupboard is the only place left and there is nowhere to hide.

Unboxing brilliance isn't easy work.

It takes deep courage to shed off patterns, paradigms, habits and identities. Expectations and tacit cultural agreements don't peel away with ease.

Bursting through the wall of each box can leave you with bruises, so my advice is this: Take time, take a beat, take a breath.

When the air feels sucked from your lungs, take a moment to acclimatise.

Remember, you don't reach new heights without altitude sickness, and putting your energetic body and mind to new limits of possibilities can have big physical effects.
Unbox, expand.

Go back to basics and repeat as often and as beautifully broken as you need to be.

Journal Prompts:

- How have your edges of darkness helped to illuminate your brilliance?

- Which dark times have turned into beacons of light?

- Have you ever had a curve-ball in life and something turned out even better than you could have planned for? What did you gain from this?

- Have you ever experienced bruises from unboxing and expanding? How did you feel?

Your Personal Power Paradigm

One of my daughters is currently learning to play the piano.

As I encourage Mia to practice, I have been assuring her that just a few minutes each day really builds up.

What's more, those super tricky bars and difficult fingering patterns get easier and easier the more we slow down, take them one by one, and keep at it. When I was younger I played the violin.

I remember that there were bars that were super tricky to master, but if I spent time working on them slowly, I could eventually rely on my fingers and brain to work together so it became a fluid connection between muscle memory and my instrument.

There are so many takeaways from learning an instrument and being part of an orchestra:

- The first play through is usually pretty awful but it always comes together for the final performance (and it's amazing)
- You need to work together as a section on the details to make the big picture work

- Controlling nerves before a performance becomes like second nature
- Theatre and appearance is part of the experience (aka, if you can't play a few notes, keep your bowing like the rest of your section and no-one will know)

So, what's the point here?

We all have so many experiences in life that give us unique insights.

We may not immediately equate a non-professional experience with what we 'do', but it is, of course, all unboxed and connected.

Working as a writer gives me a unique viewpoint, as does my experience as a designer, a consultant, an artist, a waitress, a yogi, a mum of twins, an invisible illness warrior, a meditator, and a vegan.

Every single project, experience or role that we partake in has valuable takeaways, and many experiences that we subconsciously bring to how we operate and how we serve others.

It's easy to discount your backpacking stint as irrelevant to your work, or to wonder how on earth your part time job at a retail store can have any bearing on how you roll in your professional life now.

However, by looking at your life experience, skills, and choices, and choosing to unbox them with fresh eyes, we really get a sense of just how unique and powerful your lens on life is.

I call this your Personal Power Paradigm.

It's the baseline on which you build everything else; when you really dig into the depths of experiences and skills you already have. Truly, it's an incredibly powerful exercise.

You can begin to see out-of-the-box connections of how to really make your approach aligned with your values and natural way of being.

You also find a profound sense of reassurance and confidence that you are already enough, and that you have SO much to offer.

My client, Rachel Foy of *The Soul Fed Woman (https://www.soulfedwoman.com/),* discovered exactly that as we worked together in a Brilliance Reloaded programme. I walked the group through how to tap into their brilliance, and for Rachel, the Personal Power Paradigm unlocked so much for her that it really boosted her confidence and helped to hone her message.

She says:

'That was the catalyst for me to actually own my brilliance For me, I felt that shift of completely trusting and believing that I've got what it takes to do what I need to do.'

Rachel had started to lose trust in herself (maybe you can relate? I know I certainly can!).

She thought she was doing something 'wrong'; she wasn't capable, or not brilliant enough to shine in her business, because something just wasn't clicking properly.

Doing the Power Paradigm exercise showed her that she was already equipped with what she needed, that she had everything to hand already.

As Rachel says, working through the Power Paradigm exercise was like a lightbulb moment for her: 'I was like, 'Oh, actually, I've got everything. I've got what it takes. I now need to own it.'

Rachel's story is typical of many people I work with. Everything can seem right on paper, but when something isn't clicking, it's often that these wonderful people haven't given themselves permission to own their brilliance, simply because they haven't connected to it fully themselves.

Re-connecting them to it is like a spark plug igniting an engine to start gaining some motion. It's truly magical to witness, and one of the reasons I love this simple exercise so much.

Susanne Schwameis had a similar outcome from working with the Personal Power Paradigm exercise. Susanne mentors women entrepreneurs to soar past their income ceiling and create legacies with their wealth (https://www.susanneschwameis.com/).

Her biggest mindset changes from our work together were all to do with going from imposter syndrome and 'feeling like I have nothing to say', to trusting her unique point of view to contribute to the conversation. In what Susanne calls the 'vast sea of online coaches/businesses', she now knows how to stand out and what makes her different.

That shift is huge, and it can be as simple as just journaling on some key prompts.

Journal prompt:

- Choose 5 of your previous roles/experiences/hobbies and unbox them in a journal.

- Journal/list what comes to mind when you think of your approach to your work.

- Journal/list what comes to mind when you think of your expertise.

- Journal/list what comes to mind when you think of your experience (remember, this helps you to unbox).

- Journal/list what comes to mind when you think of your personality.

- What were the key takeaways?

- How can you bring some of these into your body of work now?

- What do you bring to your work that is unique?

5

Owning your brilliance

It serves no one to hide your brilliance; it's not polite to play it down, or rude to be amazing.

You are inherently awesome ☐
However you choose to shine, own it, claim it, and live it.
Shining doesn't mean being loud, inauthentic, or brash.
It's permission to be you, wholeheartedly.You got this.
She-she-she-shine on ☐☐☐ *Giff Xoxox*

One of the biggest hurdles in owning your brilliance is getting over the fact that you are ALLOWED to talk about your brilliance.

Think about it.

It's like a Fight Club loop (except I DO want you to be talking about it).

But here is the block:

'No-one likes a show off,'.

Ever had someone tell you that?

Maybe it was a teacher.

Maybe it was a parent, or a parent figure.

Maybe it was a kid at school. Or a sibling. Or a friend.

Or...the list goes on.

Maybe it was just society (which, by the way, applies particularly if you are a woman).

Somehow we have all been taught that only show-offs talk about how brilliant they are. Only people who are arrogant, conceited, or 'above themselves'.

Can you think of someone who said that to you, or even made you feel like that?

Now, I want to start unpacking that belief.

Think about someone whose work you really, really admire.
Someone who has made a huge difference in your life.

That person shared their brilliance with you, right?

They made an impact on you. They may have even changed your life.

That's what sharing your brilliance is really about.

And guess what, someone out there needs yours.

Let's change the narrative about show-offs, shall we?

Owning your brilliance can be a tricky mode to step into, as it goes against all the things we have been indoctrinated to edit about ourselves.

(Side note: I created a challenge to help you do just this. It's called the Own Your Brilliance Challenge https://www.jogifford.co/brilliantyou).

But when you do start to own your brilliance, to unbox it and share it with the world, wonderful things start to happen.

That wonderful alignment of who you are and what you bring to the world pings up in all sorts of places - the work you do, the people you meet, the situations you experience.

Why? When we know ourselves better, it becomes far, far easier to be selective about what we say yes to, what we say no to, who we spend our time with, how we plan our days (and, therefore, our lives).

When we know ourselves better, we bring more of our true selves to every interaction we have with family, friends, clients and colleagues - and that authenticity is refreshing.

Your voice is so unique, you have a unique lens on the world, and when you begin to realise how to articulate that and embody your values?

Well, that's when the magic begins.

Your own brilliance is a not-so-secret weapon from resorting to the #samesame BS we so often see in the world.

When you know you are beautifully brilliant, you don't need to:

-   Plagiarise

-   Adopt a new persona that feels unaligned

-   Try too hard

-   Get shouty to be seen and heard

-   Go controversial

-   Be led by tactics

You are already brilliantly you.

Knowing your own power paradigm brings a confidence that transcends the soup of #samesame.

Here is an example as a story, which might resonate with you.

Recently, I dropped my kids off at a birthday party with one of their friends who lives on a farm.

As I went to stroke my daughter Eva's hair and give her a hug, I felt my engagement ring come flying off...into a snow-laden driveway.

Oops.

I had been meaning to get it re-sized - it's an heirloom gifted by my partner's Nan - but hadn't gotten around to it.

As more and more party dropping parents arrived, they found a growing group of us searching in the snow for my diamond ring.

One super smart thinker came out with some buckets of water so the snow would melt and make the search easier - but we still couldn't see it.

I knew it hadn't gone far.

But then, as more of us were searching and it seemed futile, I started to question myself; did I really feel it drop? Was I SURE I was wearing it?

I had to keep calm and really assure myself that I KNEW it was there.

After around 20 minutes, we found it.

Relieved, I burst into tears, and promptly went to visit a jewellers to ask about re-sizing.

Finding a sparkler in the snow isn't easy.

It reminds me so much of how we sometimes feel about our own genius.

We are sure it's there, but the more people that come to help, the more we may feel foolish as it seems harder to see.

But it IS there.

Shining. Sometimes hidden, waiting to be re-discovered.

And people ARE here to melt that snow and help you find it, no matter how frustrated and worried you might never see it again.

Journal Prompts:

- Can you recall a time when you have been asked to tone down or be humble about something? How did it make you feel?

- Knowing yourself as you do now, how can you start to own your brilliance a little more, right now, today? It might be as simple as reminding yourself to say 'thanks!' when someone pays you a compliment, or it might be a bolder move to share your brilliance (the Own Your Brilliance Challenge will help here too).

- Have you ever felt like your genius was in hiding? If so, how did you find it?

- Revel in your own awesome.

Living your brilliance

She knew she was able to fly because when she came down
She had dust on her hands from the sky, she said I touched a cloud
She felt so high, the dust made her cry
She knew she could fly like a bird but when she said
'Please raise the roof higher' nobody heard they never noticed a word
The light bulbs burn, her fingers will learn

Polar Bear, Ride

Brilliance is a funny one.

Often you don't realise you are revelling in your brilliance of acting in your highest power because it's just what you *do* on a daily basis.

Your brilliance seems like normality to you but to other people, what you say, how you act, or how you behave might inspire them. It offers something else to their lives that you don't see.

One of the best ways to start to unpack what your brilliance is to ask other people - yep, quieten down that inner voice that probably just piped up. Asking for feedback is totally normal in any kind of development, both personal and professional. We just happen to be hardwired to think it's selfish, narcissistic, or over indulgent.

Let's change that right now.

Simply asking a selection of friends, peers, colleagues and family members what they enjoy about spending time with you, or the conversations you have together, can be such an illuminating experience.

Make it part of your feedback and reflection in your working life as well to be asking your client about the reasons they come to you, and what is it about you that attracted them to you in the first place.

This all feeds into defining what your USP is, and when you get super clear on your values and how other people perceive you, you can start to piece together where your brilliance truly lies (but most importantly, to see it for yourself).

You shine in your brilliance all the time without realising it.

You have a special mix of talents, skills, expertise, insights, character traits, humour, and quirks, all those amazing things, that I call your paradigm baseline, which nobody else has.

Nobody else has that unique mixture of all those things that make you you.

Start to ask around and to delve in further (remember, I invite you to take my *Own Your Brilliance 10 Day Challenge* to start to really uncover what it is that makes you super brilliant).

Asking for feedback is important. But asking for validation and seeking it in the wrong places can be super harmful.

Feedback is the honest and unbiased critique of our words, actions, and behaviour. Validation is quite different, and it usually comes from our need to feel seen, to feel worthy, to belong, and to be 'enough'.

So, I have a question for you:

From whom do you seek validation?

When we talk about brilliance, who do you want to see yours?
Who do you hope will validate it?

It's quite a powerful question, and the answers you unpack might surprise you.

It might be a parent, a partner (or an ex), a friend, a colleague, a rival.

Recently I have been consciously redesigning and revisiting how I spend my time (and energy) on social media.

Over the last 6 months my presence on platforms has been reduced greatly - partly from being involved in projects that mean I don't actually have the time to post as often, and partly because I am taking time to be more discerning about where I seek validation from.

The culture on social media leads us to seek validation from likes, hearts, and comments - and the more I re-examine my own behaviour around digital spaces, the more jarring it is to see how fervently others (my past self included) rely on them.

Moreover, how much faith we put in other people to model behaviours, practices, and to curate their lives for us to follow.

We need to remember that there is a helluva lot of Emperor's new clothes action going on.

So why do we allow it to affect us?

Simply because we don't believe enough in ourselves.

We don't think we have anything to say, or we think that we are worth less than Person X who has shared their income with us for the 50th time this week, or Person Y who is an 'influencer'.

When you work out what your own values are and what brilliance means to you - and specifically, uniquely, you - it becomes far easier to be your own validation.

It turns out that you CAN shine and 'stand in your power' (to use a typically overused phrase) without everyone and their pet ants seeing it.

You can own your brilliance outwardly and be super selective about who gets to experience that.

It's a paradigm shift for me, an over sharing blogger who has been publicly airing laundry for about 14 years - but it's so refreshing to revisit and redefine who we seek that praise from and how time and energy can be spent.

I think impact comes from doing less, with more integrity, clarity, and focus. By simply asking the question ' who am I trying to please?' we can uncover some hidden motivators that might be skewing your efforts and your energy, so it's time for a re-align.

Whilst digging into brilliance, it's inevitable that we come to think about success and its relation to it.

This is often not from our own perceptions of what makes us brilliant, or who we are inherently; there could often be pressure around us for versions of success amongst our tribes, our peers, and our communities.

Interestingly, the more that I make a self-inquiry into what fundamentally makes someone successful, the more it appears to me that success is at a micro level, and is deeply, deeply personal.

When I look back on my daily journals, and daily reflection practice to check in on what I've achieved in any day, I can see that success for me occurs in the smallest of ways.

It occurs in finding joy, and in being with my children, taking them to the park or going for a walk. I find it in going for a bike ride or my yoga class, and being with loved ones; in successfully running meetings and participating as a leader in creating outcomes and products that have value for my client and for my teams.

Success, for me, comes in keeping a check of my mindset every day and seeing where I have learned and grown as a human being.

It also means identifying where I have yet to learn and grow, and what I can do about it.

Success for me also speaks to checking in with myself.

Every day, every week, and every month I work to ensure that I am becoming the fullest version of me, wherever possible, and as much as possible.

Success for me is not about creating a certain amount of income.

It's not about living in a certain place.

It's not about being accepted and acknowledged by any group or individual (the irony being, of course, that these things all sort themselves out when you ARE the best version of you and make a daily upgrade).

It's freeing to not have to keep up with the Joneses - whoever the Joneses might be for you.

It's freeing to unbox your version of success, and to realise that your brilliance happens in moments of the day.

It happens in moments of reflection, it happens in moments of interaction, and brilliance is often unseen.

That one interaction you had with someone could have changed their day and had a great impact.

That time you took to reflect on how you wanted to behave in a certain situation could now feed into how you deal with human conversations from here on in.

Realising that can also happen behind closed doors has been a huge one for me.

For many years I aligned achievement and recognition with success. I am sure you know the thing 'when I earn xxx I will be successful', or, 'when I am in XXX magazine, I will have made it!'.

It's been a fabulous journey to uncover how you can achieve and enjoy progression without the need to be validated by swathes of people.

You can shine a light, you can have a great impact on people in your world and in your life without outwardly telling people what you're doing every step of the way.

There are people, communities, and enclaves whose opinions don't matter to me at all, and freeing myself from that is gold dust.

Asking yourself the question, 'whose opinion matters to me?' is a powerful exercise, and can be truly transformational.

Unboxing yourself from that need to be validated, seen by, and aligned with people groups, organizations of movements, is a really freeing experience.

Your journey to becoming the most brilliant version of yourself will be different to everybody else's on this planet and that's totally okay! Unbox yourself from inherited and acquired versions of success - you are so much more than that.

Journal prompts:

- Really question what success means for you. Does success mean acceptance by any particular body of people - co workers, colleagues, peers, friends, or organisations? If so, look at each one and consider whether that validation really truly matters to you.

- Take time to reexamine your own criteria for what success means. These will align with your values, and will be inherently linked with how you live your life as the brilliant bespoke version of you.

- How do people see me? What surprised me about the answers?

- From whom have I been seeking validation? Is it a healthy motivation?

- How could I reframe my ideas about success and what brilliance means to me?

The Boxed up Work Ethic

'Blessed are the flexible, for they shall not be bent out of shape'.
— **Michael McGriffy**

We are funnelled down paths in life at so many junctures.

We have to choose:

- ☐ The one career

- ☐ The one niche

- ☐ The one industry

- ☐ The one person

- ☐ The one way to live

- ☐ The one lifestyle

- ☐ The one path

These are all narratives.

They are also all pretty dang boxlike, don't you think?

What if you chose to un-tick the boxes?

To embrace liminal identity (hat tip to Free Range Human Marianne Cantwell), to explore, to revel in multiple skills, fluid projects, creative ways to be all the things you are when you feel like being them?

The power and freedom in taking your brilliance back out of the boxes is transformational.

Sure, when things are unboxed they can get messy.

So let's dive into the mess, enjoy where it takes us, and say no to the rigidity of 'shoulds' and inherited storylines, shall we?

My diverse range of income streams has often been a source of amusement for some friends of mine that I have known since schooldays.

I am, as the fabulous <u>Marie Forleo</u> terms herself, a 'multi passionate entrepreneur'; my career path has zigzagged across design, marketing, PR, design management, new business, innovation, social media, lecturing, creativity, consultancy, blogging, copywriting and e-course creation, and project management (not including early jobs in catering and retail for pocket money of course).

At school, I found it so hard to work out which way to go.

I adored languages, art, literature, and music, and was even more shocked to find that when I chose to do a Foundation Course in Art I would have to decide again between textiles, fashion, illustration, fine art, graphics…

how can you possibly choose when you love it all?! I am sure you might feel the same.

There is a narrative being promoted at every stage of our careers and learning that you need to find the 'One Thing' to specialise in; the one style of illustrations, the one sound of music, the one form of creation, the one box to package yourself up in and sell.

I happen to think there is a heck of a lot of value and exploration to be found in mixing up how you earn your living.

My original career path began as a graphic designer, before I realised that I loved the brainstorming, new business, on the job learning, and team management elements the most. My MA in Design Management re-ignited my love of writing, and opportunities to teach along the way have been immensely enjoyable and fulfilling.

I have been self employed for the last 13 years. In that time I have had such a diverse range of jobs including travel writing commissions, social media management, print and web design, professional blogging, copywriting, project management, social media management, marketing strategy creation for huge global brands, consultancy for the Arts Council and lecturing at 3 different institutions in Cambridge and London.

So, am I jack of all trades and master of none?

In some ways, maybe, but there are key strands of innovation creativity and management that have run through all the projects I have enjoyed the most.

A portfolio career has many benefits in my unboxed opinion.

1. You don't have to settle

Being a multi-passionate entrepreneur can mean it is hard to fit into any particular job 'box'. It just doesn't work for me, and I like that. It might work for you, too.

2. You get to try out different lives

By dipping a toe in different careers and industries you are afforded an insight into alternative career opportunities. Each orientation can be like a mini odyssey of 'what if's', an insider's view of different roles and opportunities to manifest for yourself or to get involved with.

In short, it can help you work out what you *don't* want to do as well as what you *do* want to do.

3. Great for networking

By undertaking so many different roles and projects my network is naturally large. Connecting and collecting people is something I love to do, and it naturally happens when you keep evolving. You collect amazing people and insights along the way.

4. No one day is the same

Variety can be exciting, and by working on different projects your creative edge is always informed and kept alive.

5. Evolution naturally happens

As skills develop, networks change, and technology moves on, the journey of personal development is continuous. I love to learn and absorb information and skills, which happens daily as part of my myriad of projects.

My portfolio career has been exciting, inventive, formative and fun. I love to allow space for new income streams and projects that light me up, a far cry from a traditional, solid career path.

It might feel like a leap to go from a 9 to 5 to a truly unboxed way of working.

Sometimes, just being aware of the idea that it's possible can be enough to spark some momentum and movement in your life.

For me, this happened back in 2002, when I picked up a book called *SEED Handbook, The Feminine Way To Create Business*, by Lynne Franks. The way the book was written really spoke to my unboxed soul - it showed me that work can be organic, intentional, creative, and that it can be designed just the way I want it.

Seeing a glimmer of light and the shimmer of a new perspective began to open up all sorts of doors for me. I didn't jump into self-employment straight away; in fact, what that part of the journey did was to open up doors I would never have even dreamt of had I not been open to new ways of thinking. I landed a role at a company I worked for previously, but with full autonomy, much higher pay, and a lot of flexibility.

Unboxing can happen in all sorts of ways.

Similarly, your desired level of freedom in any area will be a totally personal thing. You might want to combine two or three very different skills and income streams, or maybe you are off the charts happy with a role that you love doing with a little sprinkle of flexibility and the hint of a side hustle.

Whatever works for you.

Once we begin to unbox our brilliance from the narratives of normalcy, new opportunities and ideas arise.

Staying open to them is the key.

As Ryan Holiday points out in his wonderful article 'The Case for being a multi-hyphenate':

'It's perfectly possible to be good at more than one thing in your life, or to be good at multiple things simultaneously. In fact, I would argue it's easier than people think. Ask any truly transcendent athlete or writer or investor or businessperson, and invariably you will hear them rail against hyper-specialization in one breath and in the next, tell you how being skilled at many things made them great at the one thing for which they're principally known. Expertise in one domain may help fuel excellence in another.'

One of the things I love the most about living and working in an unboxed way is the incredible privilege of gaining skills, insights, and growth, by working with some of the brightest minds on some truly exciting projects.

All of them just rocked up and made themselves known, but by being fluid and open to working creatively, seasonally and cyclically, there is space for them to do that.

Over the last 13 years of being self employed, no quarter has ever looked the same - and I am happy with that.

Are you a multi-hyphenate, liminal shape-shifter too? It's time to claim that!

Journal prompts:

- What are all the ways you have ever earned money in the past?

- What have you enjoyed about each role?

- What are some of the ways you would love to earn money in the future?

- How unboxed would you like your income to be?

- If you could paint a picture of your week that lights you up with work and play, how would that look for you right now?

- What do you love the most about being unboxed and using your brilliance without boundaries?

- To flip it the other way, what fears do you have about being unboxed (if any)?

Brilliance Blockers

No-one will listen to us until we listen to ourselves
— Marianne Williamson

Waaaaait a freakin' minute.

Did YOU put that box there?

No?

But did you step into it anyway?

Whether it's:

- Someone else's version of success

- Someone else's vision for your life

- Limitations upheld by your peers, your culture, or your mindset ... those darn boxes are easy to settle into without even realising it.

Recently, a client sent me a message.

It went like this:

THANK YOU FOR BELIEVING IN ME WHEN I STOPPED. LOVE YOU FOREVER 🖤

So is this part of the book about how awesome I am for helping someone?

Nope.

It's about what's really behind whatever you 'do' in your body of work.

As I said to my client:

'Darling, it's what I DO! I see your brilliance. I see you. And now you do too.

It's never really about content.

It's about THAT.'

Can you relate?

When we connect to our own power, we can do anything. ANNNYYYYTHING.

And that power comes from realising we are awesome at something that only WE can do.

I call it brilliance. You might call it zone of genius, your erudition, or any number of descriptors.

It's *that* feeling that you know your stuff so well, and your lens on it, that you could deliver a killer talk without any prep and drop the mic after you do it.

Your mic drop manifesto.

Now, there are lots of blockers for owning and inhabiting your brilliance.

Remember those boxes we talked about earlier on in the book? We find ourselves in them so easily - and they can block who we really want to be and what we really want to do.

Brilliance blockers can arrive in many forms.

Maybe there are people who demand more of your time and energy than you feel able to give.

Perhaps you have obligations that feel hard to negotiate right now, or to re-discover some brilliance.

Maybe you have cultural habits and expectations that are maybe well meaning, but serve to keep you small.

In my own life, I faced daily brilliance blocking from a very toxic person in my life.

My mum had a friendship with a very overpowering, dominating and toxic neighbour who arrived at our house every single day with the sole purpose of putting me and my siblings down.

My mother at the time didn't know herself how to model boundaries, so for years and years, this character ran rough-shod over my self esteem, my confidence, and my ability to form boundaries against people who took great pleasure in putting me down to make themselves feel better.

As a result, I replicated the pattern many times in my teens and adult life before I got the memo and began modelling clear boundaries for myself. When I realised this was about them, not me, it made sense. Anyone who wants to keep my gifts, my brilliance, and my happiness in a safe space is challenged by it in some way - and that's on them.

It's something I remain vigilant about all the time, and recognise the signs earlier and earlier each time.

Maybe it's a relationship that is stifling you. I have my experiences of this too - giving my creative energy, support (both financial and emotional), at the cost of my own growth.

Maybe it's your mindset (and this is a big one). Stopping ourselves from owning our gifts and our brilliance can happen for many reasons. Perhaps we just don't believe we can set and achieve goals, or we have never been exposed to the idea that it's actually ok to do that!

As a woman (albeit a white, cisgender, straight woman with all the privileges that come with that), I have still experienced many times the tacit need to be a good girl, to do what is expected by society, and to not have ideas above my station. When I was growing up, (particularly with the toxic people around me), being seen to be talented in any way was quickly knocked down with a comment about it being selfish, that I was a show-off, and a plethora of messages that amounted to keeping quiet to keep everyone happy.

Jealousy is a huge blocker for many of us who don't like conflict. It's one thing to understand on a rational level that people being unkind is an outward sign of their own inner conflict, but another to know how to deal with it, and to feel comfortable with owning our own worth, brilliance and power nonetheless.

For me, boundaries are key to all of the blockers. Whether it's distractions that suck my time and energy, like social media, family commitments, or people who aren't fuelling my life in a healthy way, boundaries have helped me enormously to reclaim my time, space, and brilliance.

Part of it comes by learning that powerful word, 'no' - and accepting that no is a full sentence, without reasons, explanations, or apologies.

I have also discovered that the more I know myself, and the more aware I am of the way our lives become more and more complicated with children to look after, older relatives to consider, social demands, work responsibilities and, of course, looking after ourselves, that cutting back on the draining things is absolutely crucial.

You might not realise, at first, that something is affecting your brilliance. I often notice it first when I come away from a conversation feeling heavier in my soul than before. I tend now to build in time before saying yes to events or invitations instantly, so I can look at what's happening around that time, check there is enough space for me to thrive, and also check in with what my gut says about it.

Learning to trust your intuition with what you fill your time with is absolutely huge in unblocking your brilliance.

Stepping into your brilliance means you need to find SPACE.

That means: gaps in your diary, time away from people, input, content, noise, THINGS.

Here are 3 things you can do right now to reclaim that crucial headspace and allow your brilliance to rock up:

1. Change how you use social media and take back control of WHEN and HOW you use it.

Reading Digital Minimalism by Cal Newport really sparked something in me. I had already been working on new habits around social media, but this book has really helped me to shape my thinking around how I can meaningfully engage with the things I want to online whilst keeping space for the big things in my planner and life.

It's been a great reminder that taking charge of how I spend my time and energy means I can carve out space for leading the projects I am working on, writing my book, diving into creative projects, working with my clients, being a present and mindful parent, and feeling like *me*.

2. Try Any.do or ToDoist to plan your tasks on your phone (it syncs to a Chrome version too).

I find that taking a moment to set priorities for my day helps my brain stay free from clutter (believe me, there is a LOT of clutter in there!)

Plus, I can add reminders to lists, update what I need to do for work and personal stuff, and radically reduce the cognitive overload and energetic baggage in my brain.

3. Experiment with time away from *other people's minds.*

This means TV, radio, podcasts, social media, audio books, all of it. It's incredible how often we are plugged in, and we are often not even remotely aware that we are listening to someone else. Allowing silence and time alone encourages some of your own best thoughts and ideas to emerge. That's your brilliance, right there; let it emerge in the spaces.

For more, you can also jump into my free Time Take Back Toolkit right here to get some practical strategies in place and reclaim your brain.

Journal prompts:

- Can you identify some key brilliance blockers from your life as a child? Who tried to hold you back? What would you say to them now?

- What is blocking your brilliance right now, in this moment?

- How can you reclaim some space for your brilliance?

- What boundaries do you need to put in place?

Going beyond the boxes

'You have brains in your head. You have feet in your shoes. You can steer yourself any direction you choose. You're on your own. And you know what you know. And YOU are the one who'll decide where to go...'
— Dr. Seuss, Oh, The Places You'll Go!

As we start to unbox our brilliance and step into new possibilities, understanding how identity shifts happen can be really key in making them happen much faster.

For example, in my twenties I was someone who would drink pretty much every day after work.

Although I was active and would visit the gym every morning before I went to work, would run in my lunch hours, and would often cycle most days and on weekends, I had a very unhealthy drinking habit.

I also smoked, and I had a lot of self-sabotaging habits around food, my relationships and how I lived my life in general.

I was not living in my full brilliance.

I didn't know how to set boundaries around people I spent time with.

I spent time with toxic people, I put food and substances into my body that weren't good for it, and I stunted my possibilities by making bad choices.

Fast forward to now; in my forties, I am a plant-based, yoga-loving, morning-raving, self-proclaimed introvert who really knows herself.

I know what I need, I know who I am, and whilst I'm always seeking to unbox more layers of my brilliance, I have a set of decisions around my identity and behaviours which allow me to live more easily as my true self.

So what does that mean?

Every time you make a decision, subconsciously you make it based on the identity you believe that you have.

You might have a story that is related to who you are as a human being.

Think back to the boxes; are you arty or sporty? Are you fat or thin? Are you outgoing or shy? All these labels that we apply can often become identities that are difficult to shift.

When we connect to our true brilliance and start to see the possibilities for who we really are authentically, we can connect with a different identity.

This in turn shapes behaviours, because when we know who we are, we make decisions based on that identity, not our current one.

Short-cutting that process is something I have learned to do over the years.

For example, I make a decision now based on the habits I currently have, the outcomes I want, and the identity I align with.

This makes it really easy to eliminate social groups, business circles, and invitations that don't align with me, who I am right now, and who I want to be.

I find it easier now to make a decision about what I'm going to do, and then the decision fatigue is eliminated.

If I know that I'm not drinking, I say no to a drink.

If I know that I'm not eating meat or consuming dairy, then I say no to those foods.

Once I realised that I have the permission and the keys all the time to alter my behaviours to step into my new identity, the whole thing became a lot easier. And it will for you too.

Whatever your goals are, whichever version of yourself you are looking to step into, connect with how your brilliant, unboxed self lives and behaves, and make decisions based on that identity, rather than from your past one.

For example, do you see yourself in the future as someone with loads of energy, who is confident, who leads a company, who travels, who is surrounded by friends and family?

Then make decisions based on those things.

Say no to a boozy two weeks away that takes you away from family and also reconnects you with bad habits.

Say no to all the things that are going to stop you from doing that.

You now have a decision matrix based on a future identity.

But, how can you connect with the future version of yourself to get stuck into your brilliance?

The method of creatively visualising your future self is really key to step into that identity. This is something that I have done often in the past, and it is a widely known technique in the personal development space.

My Bombastic definition of success:

- Having lots of flexible time with my family

- Earning enough money / receiving money to support a flexible, abundant lifestyle

- Making the most of and constantly exploring my abilities with an attitude of compassion, growth, discovery, and joy.

- Continually expanding my confidence, experiences, and conversations.

- To make a difference in the world in a substantial way to other people's lives.

- To use my gifts, my brain and my experiences in a way that brings joy to me and those around me.

- To feel confident in my ability to say yes and no to opportunities, people, places, as I so wish.

- To bring my family up with love, freedom, opportunity, and the spirit of creativity and exploration.

- To have the combination of travel and the chaos/experiences that it brings, alongside the sanctuary and stability of a home (or two!).

How will I know if I am successful?

- I will feel my heart starting to soar with possibility and growth.

- My belief in myself will be 100%.

- I will be a recognised thought leader.

- My self-confidence will be rising higher and higher.

- Money will be there, but it won't be the main focus or driver anymore.

- I will start to be quoted and cited everywhere, and I will feel proud.

- My income will be such that our whole family can be supported comfortably to live in the social, flexible way we choose to.

- I will recognise the person I wanted to become.

- My inner mentor becomes more and more like me.

What does she do?

- She reads, she walks, she cycles places, she runs, she enjoys dancing.

- She sings, she still goes to gigs, she meets up with friends often.

- She knows a checklist is not a guide to how her soul feels.

- She holds family close to her heart.

- She reads books, switches off from the internet craziness to drink juices and wine, and to meditate, socialise, rest, recoup, create.

- Her paintings are amazing.

- She always wanted art to be a huge part of her world, and here it is.

- She has time for yoga, painting, and her books she writes with the research to go with them fill her life with joy.

- Her children adore her - they love to sit and talk as she cooks amazing food, tries new recipes, enjoys local organic veg and new, gorgeous and glorious ingredients.

- She drives and travels for her work. She LOVES to fly, and adores the conferences she speaks at, but loves to come home and be earthed again.

- Her sense of home is strong.

- She has a mentor (or two), a counsellor, a personal trainer, yogi, daily housekeeper, gardener, and she loves to spend time down her allotment.

- She has the free spirit of an 18 year old.

- She has suffered, loved, learned, lost, and rerisen.

- She explores, and thrives on new experiences.

- She is a mentor, nurturer, creator, designer of her life and her choices.

- She is published as an author, recognised as a thought leader, and renowned for her ideas.

- She lectures, podcasts, guest hosts, writes for publications, blogs, books.

- She changes people.

- She is wise, she has learned, developed, worked, made choice after choice after choice.

She loves herself.

She loves her life.

She inspires those around her.

She could have been anything - and she is everything in one.

There was a time in 2016 when I looked at myself in the mirror, and saw, staring back at me, the inner mentor I had visualised in that exercise.

It was truly incredible to realise that I had literally stepped into that creative visualisation I set up for myself and was starting to become her.

I continue to grow into her every day (in fact, whenever I re-read that note it's uncanny just how much!)

Connecting with what the future version of you - the older, wiser even *more* brilliant version of you has to say - is so powerful.

There are a number of ways that you could do that.

Firstly, you can write yourself a letter from future you to present you.

To do this, follow these steps:

1. Find a quiet space and calm your breath.

2. Imagine yourself in the future as the older, even more brilliant version of you.

3. Really connect to her - what is she wearing, how is she standing? How does she hold space?

4. Begin to write from her to you in the present day.

5. What does she want you to know?

6. How does she want you to change to become the version of you that she is?

7. What does she want you to let go of?

You could also do a similar version of this exercise by writing to the version of you right now from some years back.

This is such a powerful way to help you see how far you have come, how much you have already progressed your brilliance, and how much you have changed.

Often, we spend so much time looking forward, it becomes difficult to see exactly how far we have already come, and it can be a really powerful thing.

1. Take a moment to once again stay quiet.

2. Take a breath and connect to the past version of you.

3. Imagine yourself in a time when things were really difficult; perhaps at a pivotal point in your life, and you just didn't know which way to turn.

4. Picture yourself in that situation and remember how you felt.

5. Now, write yourself a letter from you right now to that version of you.

6. What do you know now that she didn't know?

7. What happened afterwards that changed the course of your life?

Journal prompts:

- What does your future self want you to know, do, and see?

- What did past you reveal?

- How did it feel to connect to future and past you?

- What habits does your future brilliance self have?

- How can you start to implement those right now?

Brilliance Unboxed

The habits of brilliance

Particles change when they are observed.
We are no different. We run faster when someone is watching.
But, as you unbox your brilliance, be mindful of the audiences you choose.
Be your own observer.
Be the unicorn in the corner, happy to be acknowledged and seen by yourself, for all that you are.
Cliques come and go.Who and what is in vogue changes.
There is a huge joy and happiness in acknowledging yourself, and not the approval of others.
Be your own cheering squad.
And when someone really sees you? That's a huge bonus.

Love, the unicorn in the other corner.
Jo Gifford

Unboxing your brilliance is an ongoing, lifelong journey of discovering new ways in which to feel expansive.

It's an ever evolving exploration of being optimally, awesomely, and ultimately yourself.

Creative thinking helps us to do exactly that, and is a key part of filling up your brilliance well.

Thinking outside the box is really key to your own unboxing.

(Which is kinda obvious, I suppose. But do bear with me).

Thinking in different ways helps us to step outside those very boxes that we find ourselves in; it allows us to step aside, to investigate, question, and kick the tyres a bit in our exploration.

Thinking creatively helps us to step outside those neural pathways that we are so used to.

Thinking creatively helps us to step outside cultural norms, self-imposed limits, societal, tacit agreements.

This is where creative thinking will help you.

Igniting your brilliance in order to unbox your brilliance even more is a set of habits.

It's about finding power moves to change your perspective on a daily basis.

Some key habits to set up are:

- Doing something new every day

- Outputting every day

- Learning to find your flow

Let's take a look at each of these, and why they help you to stay out of the box and, importantly, in your brilliance.

Doing something new every day

This is a key part of keeping out of boxes (those pesky things can pop up all over the place, can't they!).

Have you ever noticed how, when we have the same actions for each day we go on autopilot?

Maybe you drive to the gym without thinking about it, you stop at the same café on the way home, you cook the same meal on a Tuesday - doing the same things over and over have us stuck in a rut.

Now, that's not to say that all repeated habits are bad. Far from it.

After all, embedding habits that help us to be fit, healthy, organised and thriving are great.

I am suggesting that you build in another habit - one that is easy to do, but has a great impact in the way you see the world.

Doing something new every day causes a ripple effect.

You might read an article in a different magazine, blog, or newswire. You might order a different coffee next time you go to a coffee shop, or maybe you will listen to a different podcast.

These new things don't have to be time consuming, super bold and audacious (although if you want them to be, have at it!); they simply need to help you discover different thoughts, flavours, perspectives, cultures, colours and experiences.

Tiny tweaks can have big effects, as my clients Seema and Peter of Tap Into Flow can attest. Seema and Peter took my advice and undertook a Daily Adventure to help their creative thinking.

One day they called me, excitedly, with a profound change:

'Jo', said Seema, 'We just HAD to share this with you! We took a different route home last night, and noticed a different area of town and the changes in housing. It got us to start thinking about what our kind of ideal home would be.'

'We started daydreaming, and explored the idea of being radical and actually living in an RV, not in house. We allowed that daydream to continue, and - guess what?! We have put the payment down on an RV, we are renting out our house, and we are going to take flow on the road!'

I loved their excited voices, and the adventure they had before them (listen to Seema and Peter talk about this themselves on my podcast, jogifford.co/podcast, Episode 15 (https://www.jogifford.co/podcast/episode -

15-creativity-and-flow-with-seema-sodha-and-peter-tiejeman).

They did, indeed, take flow on the road, and it took their lives in a completely different way; all from taking a new route home.

Now, your results may not be as radical as the Tap into Flow guys.

You might be like my other client, Mags, of Swan Waters, who ordered an espresso one day rather than a latte.

It got her thinking about sizes, perspective, and it triggered a brand new blog post for her that downloaded into her head with ease.

I find that when I am making sure I do something new every day, that I feel excited, inspired, and more like *me.*

When the concept of making the effort to do something new can just feel too much, remember it can be tiny tweaks, micro steps, and see where they take you.

Outputting every day

This is as important as inputting something new, and as the perfect partner to your daily adventures.

Your output could be:

- A journal log

- A social media post

- A blog

- An audio or video recording

- Mark making, sketching, or some way of creating

You see, when we download and reflect on our own thoughts, whether publicly to other people, or privately to ourselves, we create the space to process our experiences.

By creating something, we distil and make sense of the world around us. And guess what? We notice the boxes right before we fall into them.

In fact, here is an example of a journal entry that I posted on social media, in which I noticed my unboxed-ness, where I was beginning to feel boxed up, and what caused it:

'Today, I felt unboxed and brilliant when I was with the kids this morning watching films and baking, participating in an NYC workshop this afternoon from home.

Boxes I noticed:

The need to do more and to be more for the kids.

The boxes came from:

Internal pressure and social media.

I also noticed that:

By having a loose structure of the things I need to keep me unboxed, although a paradox, it really helps as a structure toolkit to remain me and free.

You could absolutely use the same framework for yourself at first, if a loose brief to output feels too vague.

Setting up a habit to reflect on your brilliance and unboxedness is one of the most incredibly self loving, self-authoring life design moments you can do. And it takes just a few moments.

For both the daily adventures and daily downloads, a great way to easily build them into your life is to habit stack on another established habit (hat tip James Clear, Atomic Habits).

What does that mean? Simply put, it's far easier to add a new habit in your life when it is triggered by an existing one.

In practice, that might look like building in your reflection time and download after your evening meditation. Or, perhaps your reminder to do a new thing happens after your morning run, or during your lunch break.

Experiment with what works for you, and tweak and adjust as you start to feel shifts and observe results.

Finding your flow

Your 'flow' is that state when you are in your zone, when you can't stop those moments of genius from appearing in your brain.

Flow isn't forced. It's a sense of ease.

It's the moments of space, of being, of allowing ideas to form.

Flow is the space between the tech, the conversations, the wall of information, the non-stop, über connected, hyper reached world. (Brilliance Ignition, Jo Gifford)

Reconnecting with your flow is your secret weapon to feeling like yourself.

When we are in our flow, our true nature is out to play. Our brilliance is there, allowed out of the boxes, and our brains are free from the monkey mind chatter that keeps us boxed up.

So, how do we set a habit of staying in flow? It starts with noticing, mindfully, when you are in that magical state.

For me, it's when I have allowed myself the space to sit and draw, paint, or sketch. Perhaps I have some music on, a candle burning, and I am in a joy zone.

Or, it's when I am out on a walk, noticing nature, smelling the smells of the outside world, listening to birds, to my own footsteps, and feeling grounded, present, and fully myself.

It might happen at other moments too - like cooking a meal, singing along to Fleetwood Mac at the top of my voice.

To help you identify flow, let's back up just a moment, and take a look at how the Godfather of flow Mihaly Csikszentmihalyi defines it:

'You know that what you need to do is possible to do, even though difficult, and a sense of time disappears. You forget yourself. You feel part of something larger'.

Flow: The Psychology of Optimal Experience' (1990), Mihaly Csikszentmihalyi.

Powerful stuff, right?

When we forget ourselves, all the mind monkey chatter, to-do lists, worries and conventional, habitual thinking exits stage left.

What's left is openness, opportunity, possibility, curiosity - all the ingredients of brilliance unboxing.

When you start to notice those moments you are in flow, it becomes easier to get yourself back into that state, and to find it with more ease.

Whatever those moments of flow are for you, they are more than likely to be wonderful moments when the boxes are not upon you, when you are in your full energy and joy. That, right there, is a fertile breeding ground for brilliance.

Journal Prompts:

- What new things might feel great to try in your daily adventures?

- When feels a good time to experiment with the habit of downloading?

- Have you felt boxed or unboxed today, and why?

- In which moments do you feel in your flow?

11

Living Unboxed

'Be the weirdo who dares to enjoy.'
*— **Elizabeth Gilbert, Big Magic: Creative Living Beyond Fear***

As we delve more into unboxing your brilliance, stepping into all that you are, and finding ways to be more awesomely you, let's meander into the subject of what that means for your life and how your life might look.

For me, living in an unboxed way means becoming someone who thrives on flexibility, change, and the opportunity that brings.

Now, this is something I've had a love-hate relationship with for most of my life; I often crave freedom and change, whilst also fearing the uncertainty that it brings. Does that resonate with you, too?

When you live in an unboxed way and embrace different ways of earning your income, or adding impact into the world, when change comes it's a chance to find some space, to regroup, and to engage with other opportunities.

By not living in a linear, normalised way, learning to react with interest and curiosity when things begin to change is a surefire way to thrive and to engage with whatever you allow to come your way.

Surprises often come from the space created by what you *thought* was going to happen.

Now, this is not always easy to do.

We have bills to pay, families to support, wishlists of things to invest in.

Often when plans and projects change, or when the landscape of what you thought you were going to do behaves differently, it can become a stressful thing.

But in my experience, learning to lean into a challenge and to look at the gifts of every situation allows us to create from them. We can see a chance to innovate and embrace change, we can bring leadership and creativity to otherwise stressful situations.

This, in turn, leads to even better outcomes if you can wrap your head around embracing the unboxed opportunities within them.

Living an unboxed life means reaching out to change with open arms and a blank sketchbook to start creating the next chapter.

Central to being open to living life unboxed is the mindfulness of noticing when you are feeling those boxes closing in.

For me, whenever I'm starting to feel boxed in, I experience it by starting to be aware of anxiety and tiredness - perhaps there are more flares than usual of my chronic illnesses.

I start to notice dips in my soul level joy, and I experience frustration.

Sometimes I don't even realise what's happening, but when I peel back through journaling, through meditation, and through self-awareness what led to that feeling, I often discover that I have allowed myself to become boxed in to a particular area of life.

This usually happens unconsciously; perhaps by walking into saying yes to too many things, yes to the wrong things, and not allowing myself my unboxed values that I need in order to thrive.

Often, once you realise you have become boxed in, it can feel overwhelming to make some more changes(especially so if you have associations of guilt and duty and responsibility for the areas of life in which you are boxed in).

But remember, unboxing your brilliance is about creative thinking.

It's about finding creative ways to live life your way and to question the boxes in which we find ourselves in.

As I write this book, I am 42 years old, approaching 43.

I'm at an age where many of my friends and contemporaries, as well as myself, are starting to feel the pressure of being boxed.

We have young families, we have, sometimes, older relatives who depend on us, we have houses to run, jobs to go to, income to generate, homework to do, washing to be done, all the life things that can so easily swamp up 99% of your day.

Believe me, I've been here many, many times, even during the unboxing process.

Whenever I start to feel a sense of anxiety and overwhelm, (usually when I find myself crying at the smallest thing), I realise that I've allowed myself once again to get boxed in.

Often, my default reaction is to want to run, to want to book a road trip and just go on the road, explore Europe, go to Australia, just be away from this life.

But actually, when I start to look at opportunities to unbox myself in the tiniest of ways, by adjusting how I live the life I have, it makes the biggest difference.

It might mean just taking myself out for an afternoon and doing something for me, even for an hour.

It might mean just going to an art gallery and having coffee with a friend.

It might mean booking a hotel overnight and going to a morning rave all by myself.

It doesn't need to be the extreme version.

By realising that the boxes have been building back up, it's a great time to take stock, to see, to check against the areas of life that are important to me, and to marry that up with my values and to think about how to make the tiniest changes.

How we define unboxing and living an unboxed life will be different to all of us.

Also, your level of unboxing might be different to anyone else's.

The important thing is to keep asking, what if I'm playing the dream game with curiosity?

For example, whilst my work is entirely location-independent, I can work from anywhere in the world, my partner's career is currently not. And that's fine, he does what he does, and we are super happy at the moment living where we do with our kids going to school surrounded by family.

However, there's a part of me that needs to be unboxed and able to travel. So how to find that balance?

One big dream of mine is to have a camper van and travel around Europe. But how do we do that, given the constraints of what we have but also not feeling confined to a box?

The boxed-in way is to think that it's impossible.

The unboxed way is to think, what if?

So, if the completely unboxed way is to sell our house, get a camper van, travel around Europe, and that doesn't feel available to us, it's time to explore, 'what if'?

A compromise might be to get a van and go travelling on weekends, to start exploring more freedom with what we have and see where that takes us.

We still have some holidays, Easter holidays, half-terms. We have ways to experience that feeling of travel and freedom and to enjoy being outdoors with our family, without going the whole hog.

Play with 'what ifs?'

Sometimes, just the thought that you can begin to unbox your life is enough to start a whole series of incredible events in motion.

Journal Prompts

- How might you notice when you are feeling boxed in?

- What does living life unboxed mean to you?

- Is there a big dream you have that you can start unboxing in small steps?

- What examples of extreme unboxing can you think of that feel impossible, but you might be able to find an unboxing compromise or an unboxing version that feels better for you?

12

Unboxing it All with a Bow

Hey, I am Jo.

I am a mumma, partner, business owner, leader, friend, sister, daughter, truth speaker and seeker, glitter covered duvet fort builder, nerd, self care advocating, idea generating power house of ceiling smashing, early morning raving, Virgo powered, curvaceous rainbow dust.

Bold, audacious, and unapologetically me.

It takes courage to show your brilliance, and I applaud you for being here, and for daring to begin to unbox yours.

If you have been silenced for too long too, I understand and know your pain from the inside out.

When you don't own your brilliance you enable others but leave yourself behind.

When you don't realise who you are, you let others decide for you. And that, lovelies, is never for the best.

I hope our journey together in these pages has helped you to unbox your brilliance.

Show the world what you've got, your way (whether it's how the world wants it to be or not).

It takes courage, because it's personal.

Shine, little one. It's time.

To start owning your brilliance, join my 5 Day Own Your Brilliance Challenge right here:
https://www.jogifford.co/brilliantyou

What I would love most of all is to hear from you.

Let me know how this book sparked your brilliance fire - find me on social media or ping me an email. I will be ready and waiting to hear your story and to witness your brilliance unboxing.

Thank you for braving your brilliance with me. It's truly an honour.

Jo

jo@jogifford.co

Twitter.com/thejogifford

Instagram.com/thejogifford

Facebook.com/jo./jogifford

Acknowledgements

This book would not be in your hands without the magic of Nicola Humber at the Unbound Press. Thanks for holding space for me to let the book arrive as it needed to. Huge thanks to my clients, to everyone who has let me loose on their brilliance - I owe so much to you. To my magical squad of cheerleaders and soul family who have always believed in me, thank you. And to Miles, Eva and Mia, who see me and believe in me every day, and always remind me what matters - thank you. I love you. Finally, I acknowledge you, the reader. I am so grateful you chose to read these words. If it feels good to do so, spread the word. The world needs more brilliance unboxed.

Printed in Poland
by Amazon Fulfillment
Poland Sp. z o.o., Wrocław

56299080R00065